Bastien and Bastienna

COMEDY OPERA IN ONE ACT

Music by
W. A. MOZART

English Text by
HAMILTON BENZ

G. SCHIRMER, Inc.

DISTRIBUTED BY
HAL•LEONARD®
CORPORATION
7777 W. BLUEMOUND RD. P.O. BOX 13819 MILWAUKEE, WI 53213

Note

CAST OF CHARACTERS

BASTIENNA, a shepherdess ....*Soprano*

BASTIEN, her sweetheart ....*Tenor*

COLAS, *a would-be magician* ....*Bass*

Wolfgang Amadeus Mozart (1756-1791) wrote his little opera, "Bastien and Bastienne" in 1768, at the age of twelve, for a little theatre in the garden of Dr. Anton Messmer, a Viennese doctor and friend of the Mozart family, where is was first performed as an entertainment for Dr. Messmer's guests by amateurs.

The libretto was a German version by Friedrich Wilhelm Weiskern of a French operetta, "Les amours de Bastien et Bastienne," which, in turn, was based on a little 'Intermezzo" "Le devin du village" (The village seer) by Jean-Jacques Rousseau, the great French philosopher who also composed music for his play.

BASTIEN AND BASTIENNA

English text
by Hamilton Benz

Introduction

Wolfgang Amadeus Mozart

(The scene represents a village with a view of the fields.)

1. Aria

Andante. un poco Adagio   (The curtain rises)

Bastienna

I nev-er thought my love would.

leave me, And now I can - not rest or sleep, I can - not rest, I

can - not sleep.   Is it the truth? Could he   de-ceive me? So deep this

pain, I can - not weep! I feel such pain I can - not weep.

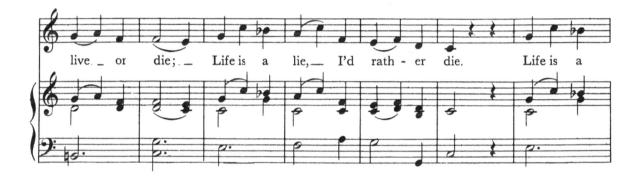

No, but I don't *want* to die. O, Bastien, you gave me your word, you swore to be true. Then you see a pretty face and you're gone. If only I could forget your name, stop thinking of you! Why do I love you so much? Love . . . love is a fool. So am I.

2. Aria

Andante

Bastienna

I walk the fields and tend to My

flock, my sheep, the ewes and rams; My flock, my sheep, the ewes and

rams. What joy to be a friend to The lit - tle new-born lambs, The lit - tle

new - born lambs. They are the

one con - so - la - tion for me. When they're near I lose all fear.

8

Then from that deep des-o - la -tion I'm free. Trou-bles— cease And I'm at

peace. They give re - lease, Trou-bles cease, I'm at

peace. When— they're near— I lose— all fear, When— they're

near— I lose—all fear.

(Colas approaches from a hill, playing a bagpipe.)

3. Aria

Allegro

4. Aria

Young girls are al-ways ask-ing— me To be their for-tune-tell-er And read the fu-ture for_____ them. Their eyes tell me just what they want: Some-one who will a-dore them. Their eyes tell me just what they want: Some-one who will a-dore them, Some-one who will a-dore them. The

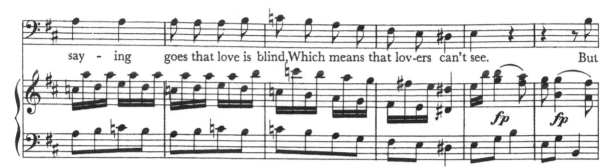

say - ing goes that love is blind, Which means that lov-ers can't see. But

fp *fp*

I can read their eyes and mind, I know what can or can't be. Yes,

fp *fp*

I can read their eyes _ and _ mind, I know _ what can _ or _

f *p* *cresc.*

can't be, I know what can or

f *p* *cresc.*

can't _____ be.

f

Bastienna: Good morning, Mr. Colas. Could you please help me?

Colas: Gladly, my dear.

Bastienna: I have a problem that's just eating my heart out, and since you're a magician you certainly can solve it.

Colas: I can solve any problem, and for something that's eating at the heart, I've got marvelous remedies. As I look into those beautiful eyes I can even read your future.

Bastienna: Really? Mr. Colas, I haven't any money but I can pay you with these earrings; they're solid gold.

Colas: Keep your earrings. From such a lovely girl as you I'll accept a very simple payment — a couple of kisses.

Bastienna: No, Mr. Colas. I'm saving them for Bastien. That is, if we're ever married. That's why I need your help because if I don't marry him I'm going to kill myself.

Colas: Kill yourself! At your age? That's silly.

Bastienna: But he's left me for someone else.

Colas: Don't let it bother you. He loves you with all his heart.

Bastienna: But then why is he unfaithful?

Colas: Unfaithful, no. Fickle, yes. He's at that age. He's also something of a materialist, likes the finer things in life.

Bastienna: And this woman is giving him lovelier, finer things?

5. Aria

Why were they such hap - py hours?___ He en - joyed___ what___

he had done.___ Can it be___ that he's en -

joy - ing What an-oth-er gives a - way, gives a - way?

What we shared he's now___ de - stroy - ing, And___ it's I who___

have___ to pay. What we shared he's now___ de - stroy - ing,

And_ it's I who_ have_ to pay. It__ is I __ who

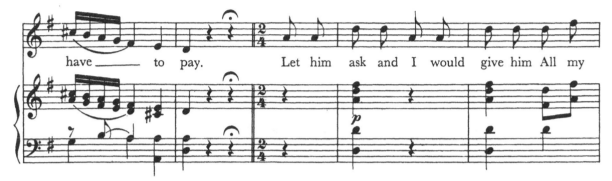

have ____ to pay. Let him ask and I would give him All my

land, my farm and sheep, All my land, my farm and

sheep. Can I pos-si-bly for-give him If he thinks my gifts are cheap? Can I

pos-si-bly for-give him If he thinks my gifts are cheap? Let him

ask and I would give him All my land, my farm and sheep. Can I pos - si - bly for-

give him If he thinks my gifts are cheap, If he thinks my gifts are cheap?

I can't bear the thought of it, The sense of shame is much too deep.

I can't bear the thought of it, The sense of shame is much____ too deep.

Colas: The point is, my dear, this lady of the manor — your rival — while using a number of feminine wiles also gives expensive presents. It's easy for a woman to have lovers if she wants to pay the price.

6. Aria

Allegro moderato

Bastienna

If I played the cour-te-san like that one, Looked for

fa - vors from all sorts of men, Old or young, the thin one or the

fat one, May-be I'd be tempt - ed now and then. No, I nev-er

would! I'm his for - ev-er. No, I never would! I'm his for - ev - er.

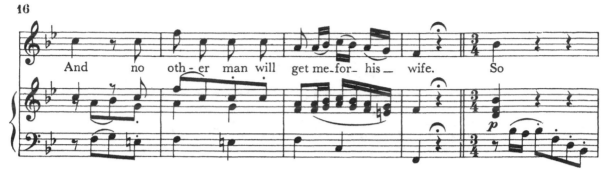

Colas: I'm in complete sympathy with those sentiments. Now as to Bastien, don't worry, he'll come back to you. But you've got to change your method, my dear. Be a little frivolous.

Bastienna: That's not easy. I can hardly talk when I'm with him, I'm so nervous. I fuss with my hair, I fix my bodice, straighten my skirt ——

Colas: What I mean is, you've got to play a game; pretend you're interested in someone else. The way to get a lover back is to go in the opposite direction — leave him.

7. Duet

This ad - vice — and do not scold me, you must-n't scold me — It is

ab - so - lute - ly__ right, It is pos - i - tive - ly__ right.

Yes, I'll think of what you__ told me, I will__ prac - tise__ day and

night, I will__ prac - tise__ day and__ night, Just for-

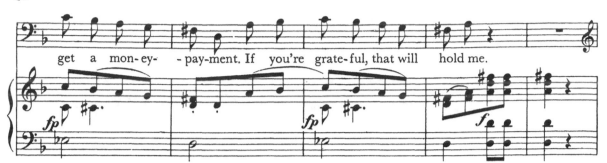

get a mon-ey- -pay-ment. If you're grate-ful, that will hold me.

Bastienna

I will work all day and night, I will work all

day and night, yes, day and night. What a sim-ple

Colas (aside)

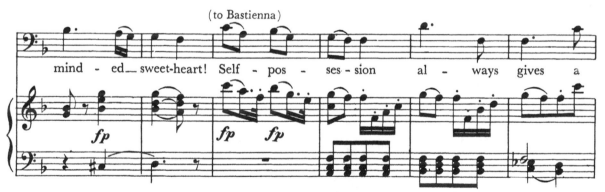

mind - ed sweet-heart! Self - pos - ses - sion al - ways gives a

(to Bastienna)

fine im - pres-sion. Show a smile to ev-'ry man. Yes, I'll

Bastienna

Colas: She's so naive, so innocent. You find this only in the country; any city girl that age knows more than her mother. But you can't tell young people anything; you can't reason with them. You have to be some sort of miracle man — then they'll listen. That's what I'll do, use some magic, give them a little hocus-pocus. Well! Here comes the boy.

8. Aria

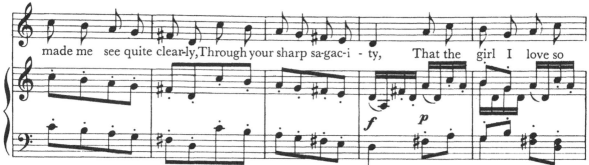

made me see quite clear-ly, Through your sharp sa-gac-i - ty, That the girl I love so

dear-ly Is the on-ly—one for— me, The on-ly girl for me.

All the plea-sures of—the— cit-y, All the

girls so rich and pret-ty, In no time at—all they—leave a— man— cold.

Bas-ti - en-na's love-ly— grace, Bas-ti - en-na's dear-est— face, Bas-ti -

en - na's-dear-est— face I can val-ue more than gold. Bas-ti - en-na's love-ly—

grace, Bas-ti - en -na's dear-est face, Bas-ti - en-na's-dear-est— face I can

val-ue more_than_gold.

cresc.   *f*

Colas: So you've come to your senses! Unfortunately it's too late.

Bastien: Too late?

Colas: You've lost her.

Bastien: I've lost Bastienna? You're joking. It isn't true. She belongs to me, she said so herself. She's not the kind of girl to give her heart to someone else.

Colas: Maybe not *give* it .But she might let it be taken.

9. Aria

That's a sil-ly piece of

fic - tion, Noth-ing else but sil-ly fic-tion. Bas-ti-en-na does-n't

cheat, She's a girl who'd nev-er cheat. That would be a con-tra-

dic - tion, Noth-ing but a con-tra-dic-tion. She could nev-er

use de-ceit, Nev-er, nev-er use de-ceit.

How I love to see her blush - ing

When she hears me say her name. Then a

fierce de - sire comes _ rush - ing, Burns me like _ a

sear - ing flame, Burns me like _ a sear - ing

flame.

Colas: That may be so. However, Bastienna has another admirer — very distinguished, rich, attractive.

Bastien: No. It can't be true. But how do you know?

Colas: I have a certain power of divination.

Bastien: I don't believe it.

Colas: Poor Bastien. You'll find it's true, soon enough.

Bastien: Why should this happen to me?

Colas: I'll tell you why. The material things in life come too easy to a handsome young man, and they tend to lead him astray.

Bastien: But I love her, Mr. Colas. This is awful. Isn't there some way I can get her back?

Colas: I'm fond of you both, I feel sorry about this and I sincerely want to see you together again. I just might be able to work out something. Let me refer to my book on magic . . .

10. Aria

Andante maestoso

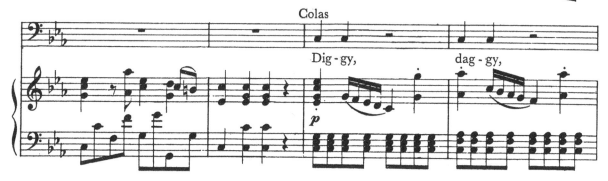

lo - rum, la - rum, Rau-di, mau-di,

gi - ri, ga - ri, po - si - to, bes - ti, bas - ti, Sa - ron - fro,

fat - to, mat - to, quid pro quo,

fat - - to, mat - - to, quid pro

quo; Dig-gy, dag-gy, scur-ry, mur-ry,

Colas: That takes care of that. Don't look upset, Bastien; you're going to see her again.

Bastien: You're sure?

Colas: Provided you're good to her. From now on, my boy, appreciate the better things in life.

11. Aria

Tempo di Menuetto

Bastien (alone)

1. How I __ long __ for her ca - ress - es, And her hand up- on my cheek.
2. Lust for __ gold __ is what be - witch - es Men of ev-'ry race and creed.

Bas - ti - en - na's love ex - press-es The __ per - fec - tion that __ I
I can __ find __ the great - est __ rich - es In her eyes __ where I __ can

seek, __ The joy __ I __ seek.   I don't long for
read __ The love __ I __ need.   Such a love is

Bastien: Here she comes. I'd better not stay. But if I run away I'll never get her back.

Bastienna: He's such a good-for-nothing! He saw me! I wish my heart wouldn't beat so fast.

Bastien: Damnation! I don't know what to do.

Bastienna: How I hate these unexpected meetings.

Bastien: I've got to do something. Bastienna! What's the matter? Why are you making such a face?

Bastienna: Who are you? I don't know you. Go away.

Bastien: What? Bastienna, look at me, please. You know me — your Bastien.

Bastienna: *My* Bastien? Oh no! Definitely not.

12. Aria

Andante

Bastienna

He told me if I'd be his true love He'd make the whole world our

own. I said, "Dear-est Bas-tien, it's you, love" The one truth I al-ways have

known. He called my face the coun-ter-part Of an-y paint-er's great-est art, And

swore it was his du-ty To show the world my beau-ty. He swore it was his

du - ty To show the world my beau - ty, To show the world my beau - ty.

Un poco allegro

It used to be he did - n't care For wom - en who were rich and fair. No - mat - ter what they'd prof - fer, He'd turn down ev - 'ry of - fer. His heart, his love be - longed to

Adagio

me, just to me, on - ly me. And now this cruel du - plic - i - ty! I

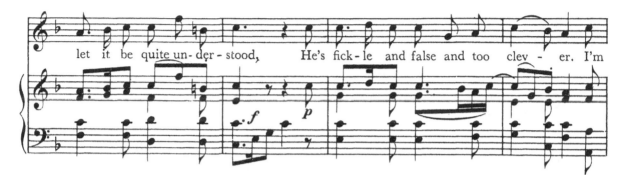

Bastien: Now I understand. You're wrong, Bastienna. I haven't changed. It's just this person — a certain acquaintance, put me under some sort of spell temporarily. But our good friend Mr. Colas used a little of his magic, and now I'm just as I was before.

Bastienna: I doubt that. But if your spell was temporary, mine's permanent and nothing Mr. Colas can do will help.

Bastien: I know what will help: marriage. A good husband is the

Bastienna: Not for me. Marriage is trouble. Add to that an unfaithful husband and you're miserable.

Bastien: That's silly.

Bastienna: It's the truth.

Bastien: You're being stubborn.

Bastienna: I'm making sense.

Bastien: If that's the way you feel, I'm going.

Bastienna: I'm going too.

13. Duet

I know a ver-y weal-thy la-dy, And I'm in-vit-ed to her par-ty;

And I can live just like a la-dy, And ev'ry night there'll be a par-ty:

We'll turn the whole place up - side down, — We'll turn the

I'll wear a dif - f'rent brand - new gown, — Each night a

Grazioso, un poco allegretto

whole place up - side down.

dif - f'rent brand - new gown.

Grazioso, un poco allegretto

She knows how deep-ly I ad - mire her;

And if I meet a hand-some squire, —

Marriage is what we both desire. She knows how deeply

I'll marry him if I desire. And if I meet a

I admire her; Marriage is what we both desire,

hand-some squire, I'll marry him if I desire,

we both desire, we both desire.

if I desire, if I desire.

Adagio

I'll

In

Allegro

share her gold and sil - ver piec - es, And I'll be just as rich as

cit - y life there's lots of chanc - es, At din - ners, par - ties, balls and

Allegro

Croe - sus! And she's a _ pa - tron - ess of art.___ I'll

danc - es, To meet a _ hun - dred weal - thy men. ___ In

share her gold and sil - ver piec - es, And I'll be just as rich as Croe - sus!

cit - y life there's lots of chanc - es, At din - ners, par - ties, balls and danc - es,

And she's a pa - tron - ess of ___ art. I have her

To meet a hun - dred weal - thy ___ men. I'll mar - ry

38

Bastienna: So . . . you're still here? I thought you said you were going?

Bastien: I *am* going. Right now.

Bastienna: Well then, go. Why is it so difficult to leave me when it's so easy for you to be unfaithful
unfaithful to me?

Bastien: This is all — a little mixed up.

Bastienna: *I'm* not mixed up. You can come or go as you please.

Bastien: If it pleases me to stay, and I ask if I can stay, will you say yes?

Bastienna: Yes . . . no . . . *No!*

14. Recitative and Arioso

walk you down the path And watch while you en-joy your bath.

Bastien: But do I have the courage to drown myself?
Bastienna: I'm sure of it. Try.
Bastien: I don't know... I was just thinking, I'm not a good swimmer. Then, too, before I commit suicide we ought to have one last talk.
Bastienna: No.
Bastien: No?
Bastienna: No! I won't listen to a word you say.

15. Duet

Allegro moderato

Bastienna

Go, go. You can't be trust-ed. I'm so dis-gust-ed.

This is the ver-y end. You can't be trust-ed. Look for an-oth-er

friend. I tell you frank-ly, it's the end; Go find your-self an-oth-er friend.

You'd love _ an- oth - er one. I suf - fer as I ought,

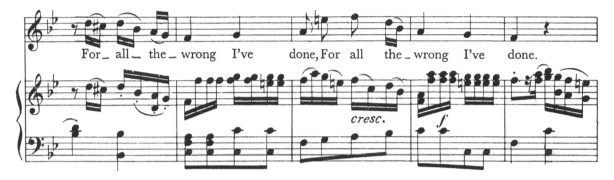

For _ all _ the _ wrong I've done, For all the _ wrong I've done.

Bastienna

Bastien

Bas-tien, Bas-tien! Yes? What is it? Why d'you call me?

Bastienna

I look at you, look in your eyes, But I don't have that hap-py _

Bastien

feel-ing. Where is that cer-tain look That made you so _ ap - peal-ing? What-ev-er

did we do to lose those hap-py days, Those mag-ic mo-ments when our love was

Adagio

Bastienna

all a-blaze? Where are those hap-py days? We'll nev-er have them, nev-er. They're

We'll nev-er have them, nev-er. They're

Adagio

gone from us for - ev - er, Gone, gone, van - ished for - ev - er.

gone from us for - ev - er, Gone, gone, van - ished for - ev - er.

I feel so bad-ly; But sad-ness_nev-er_ helps. New hap-pi - ness_will

I feel so bad-ly; But sad-ness nev - er helps. New hap-pi - ness will_

I love you more. I prom-ise you I wor-ship you, I swear I do, I

I've nev-er felt such hap-pi-ness as this! I've nev-er known such

swear I do!

ec-sta-sy, such bliss, Such ec - sta - sy as

this!

We'll be to-geth-er In all kinds of weather, And nev-er a -gain will we Ar - gue or

dis - a -gree. I'll be true just to you, on - ly

you.

There'll be no fight-ing, No

16. Trio

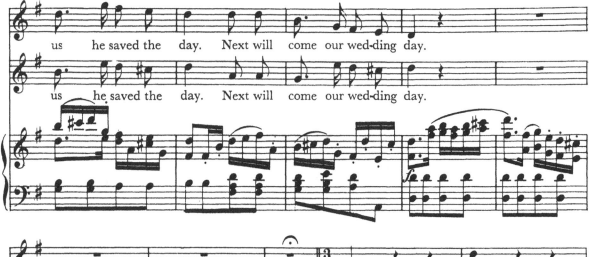

us he saved the day. Next will come our wed-ding day.

us he saved the day. Next will come our wed-ding day.

So let's

So let's

give him a cheer. He's a — man — you can't dis-

give him a cheer. He's a — man — you can't dis-

par - age. So let's give him a cheer

par - age. So let's give him a cheer

for our — mar-riage, And that we make clear, Yes, our—

for our — mar-riage, And that we make clear, Yes, our—

mar-riage will hap-pen right here.

mar-riage will hap-pen right here.

So let's give him a cheer.

So let's give him a cheer.

Colas

So they give me a cheer.

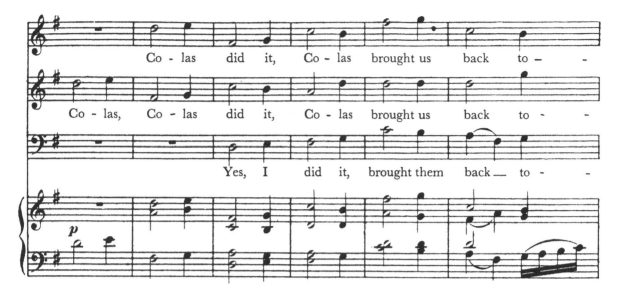

Co - las did it, Co - las brought us back to - -

Co - las, Co - las did it, Co - las brought us back to - -

Yes, I did it, brought them back to - -

geth-er. Cheers, cheers, cheers,

geth-er. Cheers, cheers, cheers,

geth-er. Cheers, cheers, cheers,

cheers! Cheer for Co - las as loud as you can!

cheers! Cheer for Co - las as loud as you can!

cheers! Cheer for Co - las as loud as you can!

Cheer for— Co - las, a won - der - ful man, a

won-der-ful man, a won-der-ful man, a won-der-ful

man!